Samuel Sailing
The True Story of an Immigrant Boy

retold by
Karl Beckstrand

For Samuel Martin Beckstrand

Samuel Sailing: The True Story of an Immigrant Boy
Young American Immigrants, Book IV (Agnes's Rescue [I], Ida's Witness [II], Anna's Prayer [III])

Text & Illustration Copyright © 2021 Karl Beckstrand. Special thanks to Marian Martin and Todd Martin
Premio Publishing, Midvale, UT, USA
Library of Congress Control Number: 9781951599126, ebook ISBN: 978-1005346508, ISBN: 979-1951599126
All rights reserved. This book, or parts thereof, may not be reproduced or shared in any form—except by reviewer, who may quote brief passages or sample illustrations in a printed, online, or broadcast review—without prior written permission from the publisher. Derechos reservados. Queda prohibida la reproducción o transmisión de parte alguna de esta obra, sin permiso escrito del publicador.

ORDER direct (hard/soft/ebook) or via major distributors.
FREE/Gratis multicultural ebooks, online secrets & lesson plans:
KidsWorldBooks.com

Other titles by Karl Beckstrand:
Horse & Dog Adventures in Early California: Short Stories & Poems
The Bridge of the Golden Wood: A Parable on How to Earn a Living
Ma MacDonald Flees the Farm: It's not a pretty picture...book
She Doesn't Want the Worms! – ¡Ella no quiere los gusanos!
Crumbs on the Stairs – Migas en las escaleras: A Mystery
No Offense: Communication Guaranteed Not to Offend
Sounds in the House – Sonidos en la casa: A Mystery
It Came from under the High Chair: A Mystery
It Ain't Flat: A Memorizable Book of Countries
The Dancing Flamingos of Lake Chimichanga
GROW: How We Get Food from Our Garden
Bright Star, Night Star: An Astronomy Story
Polar Bear Bowler: A Story Without Words
Arriba Up, Abajo Down at the Boardwalk
Bad Bananas: A Story Cookbook for Kids
Butterfly Blink: A Book Without Words
Great Cape o' Colors - Capa de colores
Gopher Golf: A Wordless Picture Book
Why Juan Can't Sleep: A Mystery?
Muffy & Valor: A True DogStory
To Swallow the Earth
God Adores You

My name is Samuel Charles Percival Martin, and I was born December 1, 1904 in Woodstock, Cape Town, South Africa. I am the oldest boy in a close family with eight children.

WEDDING DAY 23 NOV 1897

I was named after my father, Samuel Martin. My parents fell in love while working in London, England. In 1896 my father sailed to South Africa to make a life for himself. He soon wrote to my mother, Clara, asking her to come and be his wife. She accepted.

My oldest sister, Clara Emily, died before I was born. She was just a baby.

Saturday afternoon drive with family 1907.

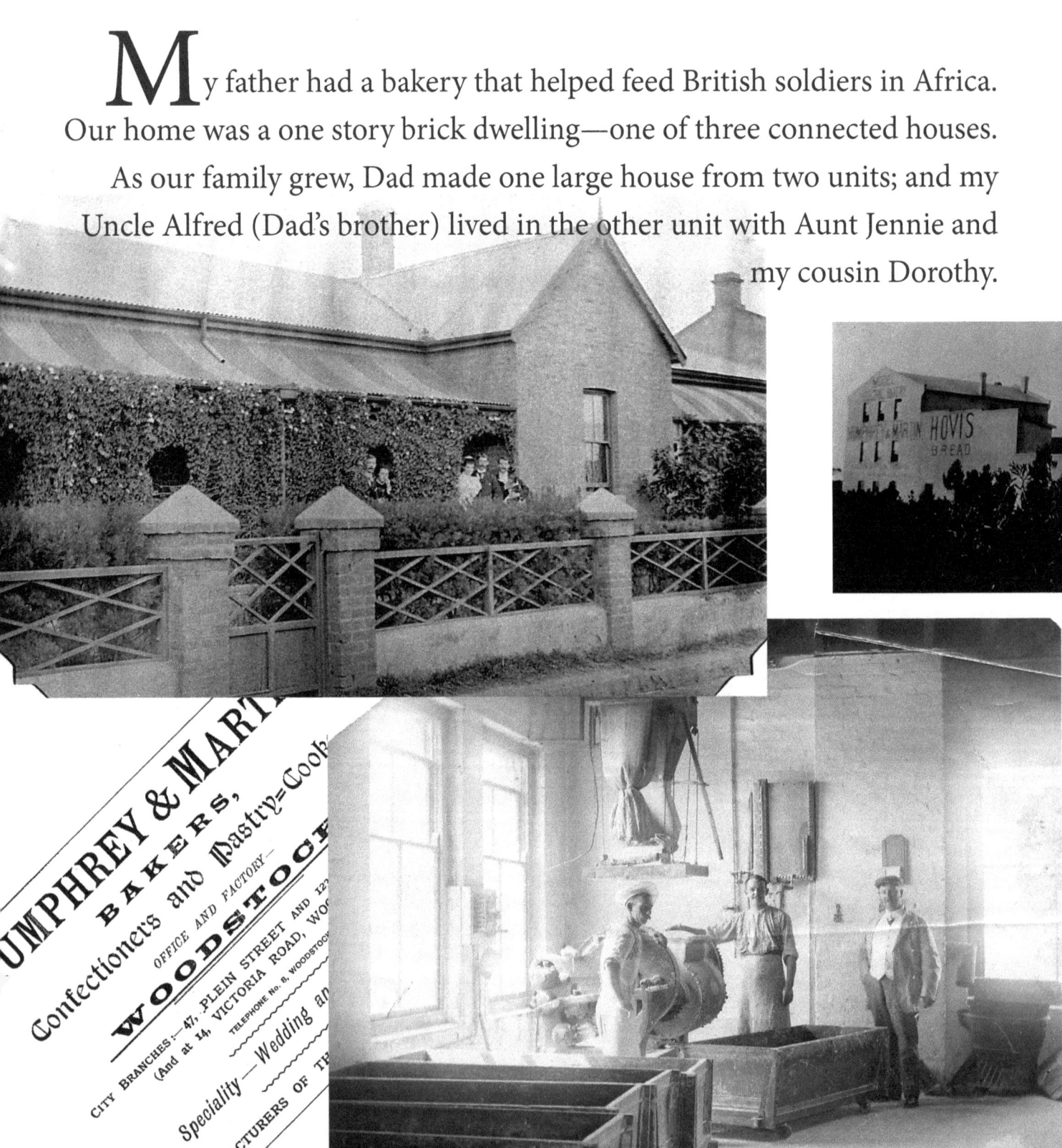

My father had a bakery that helped feed British soldiers in Africa. Our home was a one story brick dwelling—one of three connected houses. As our family grew, Dad made one large house from two units; and my Uncle Alfred (Dad's brother) lived in the other unit with Aunt Jennie and my cousin Dorothy.

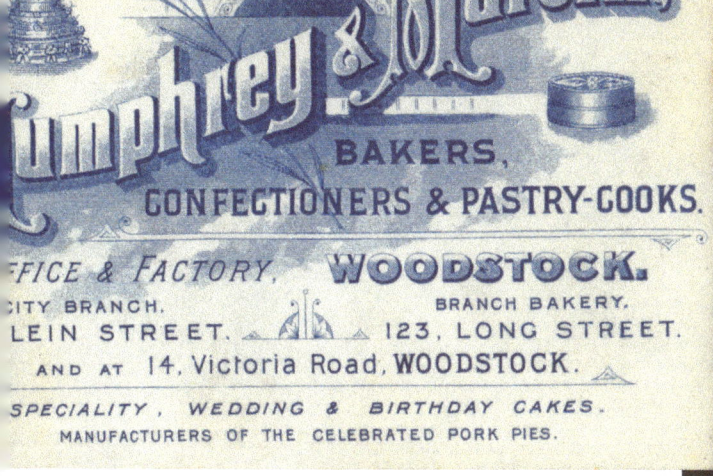

Our bakery, Humphrey & Martin, was at the end of these homes.

Our family gathered regularly for family home night. Father would read us a scripture, or he or Mother would tell about their early lives in England.

Theo, Doris, Mabel, Samuel, Jim, Clara, Ethel, and Sam

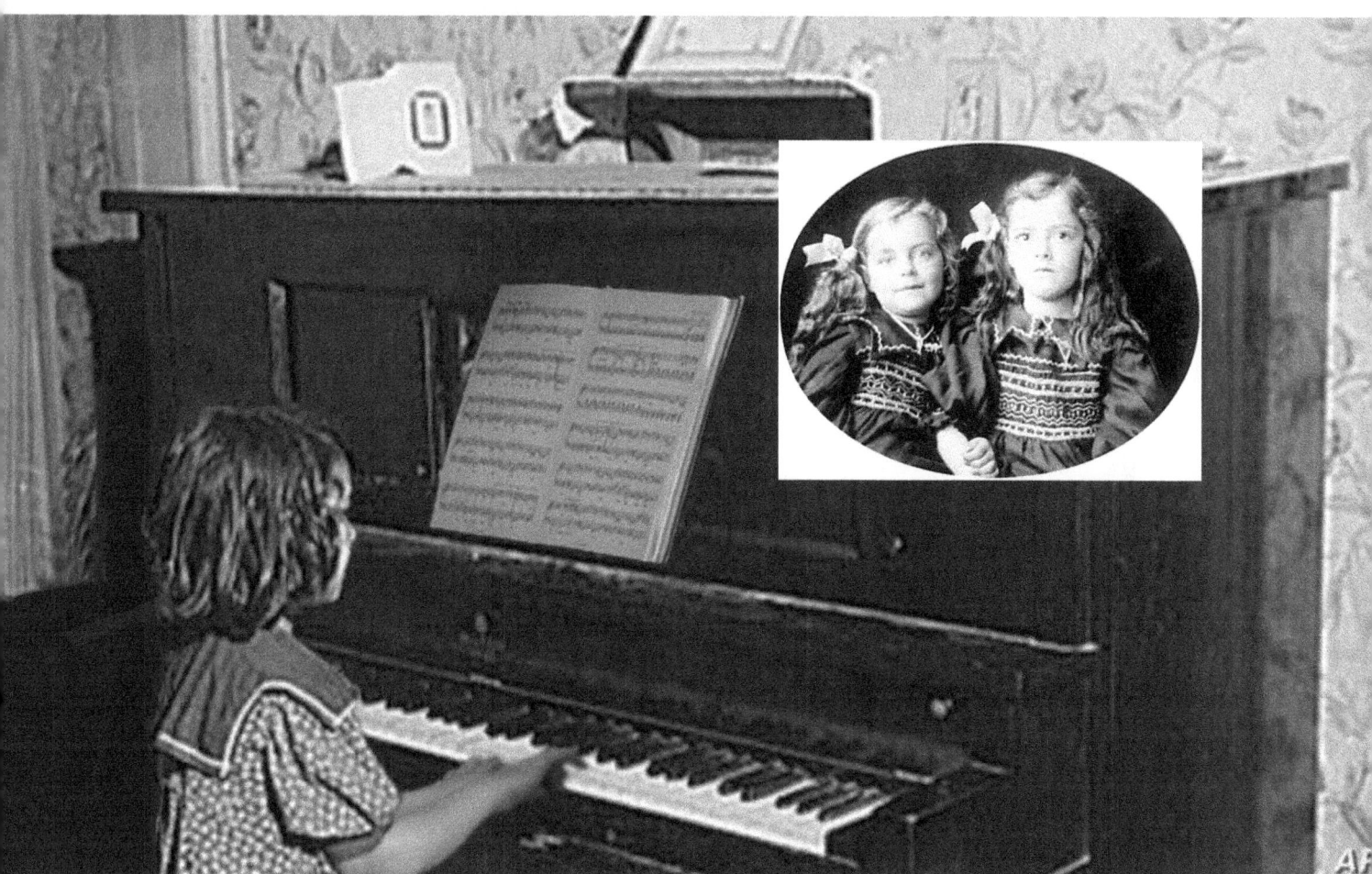

My sisters would then sing or play the piano. They were quite talented. The best part was the cake, custard, or plum pudding afterward! It was pretty important to our parents that we were all home on those special evenings.

We lived between the mountains and the sea—not a great distance to either. Sometimes we would have picnics and play on the beach.

On cold nights, my mother would warm our nightclothes by the fire. She often kept peppermints or chocolates in a drawer in the dining room. We could seldom resist the treats in her drawer.

We took baths in a great tub in the kitchen. I was baptized a member of the Church of Jesus Christ of Latter-day Saints in that tub when I was eight years old.

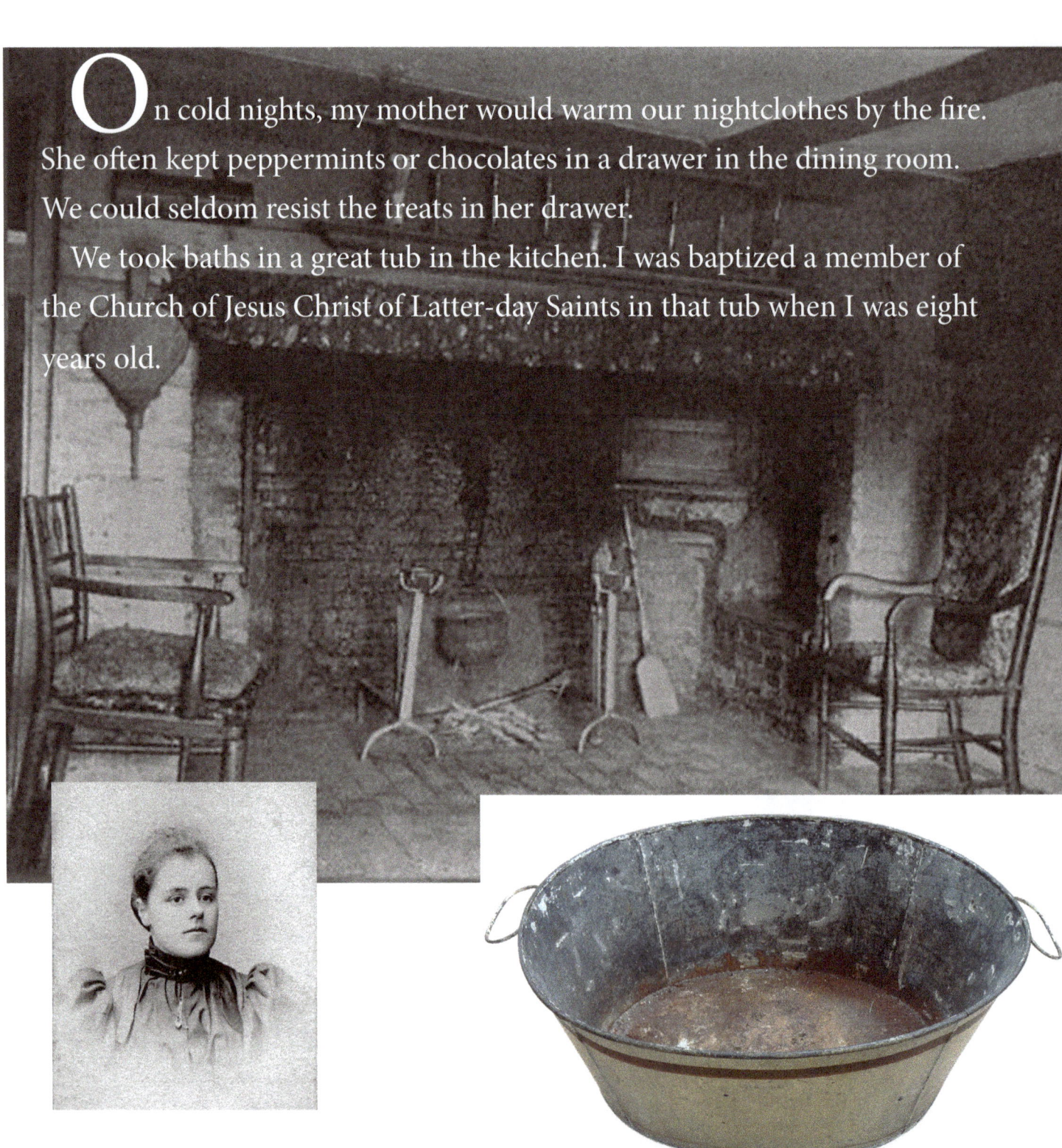

In 1913 my mother needed special medical care in England. She sailed with my siblings to London. I remained with my father for a time, and then we too sailed to England to reunite with my mother and meet my grandparents and cousins. It was a wonderful trip.

BAKERS, PASTRYCOOKS

We weren't allowed to go to the bakery very often—usually only on special errands. But it was wonderful if we were able to go on days that donuts were being made or peanuts were being roasted!

HUMPHREY & MARTIN

47 - Plein S...
123 Long...
...CAPE TOWN,
Victoria Road, WOODSTOCK

I sometimes got into trouble for sneaking into the corral and riding the delivery cart horses bare back.

TRY OUR RUSKS.

Manufacturers of the Celebrated Steak and Kidney Pies.

Noted for Wedding and Birthday Cakes.

Perfection in Hygiene Attained.

Model Electric Bakery.

HUMPHREY & MARTIN

BAKERS, CONFECTI
and PASTRY-COO
WOODSTO

Office and Factory, WOODST
CITY BRANCHES:—
99, Plein Street & 237, Long Street,

Daily Delivery—Town an

T. Harding, Son, & Co. Bristol, England.

I went to a school that was very strict. If we misbehaved we could be hit with a bamboo cane.

When I was about eleven years old my parents decided to move the family to the United States of America. Shortly after our boat passage was purchased, I got typhoid fever and was taken to the hospital. My temperature climbed to 104 degrees Fahrenheit.

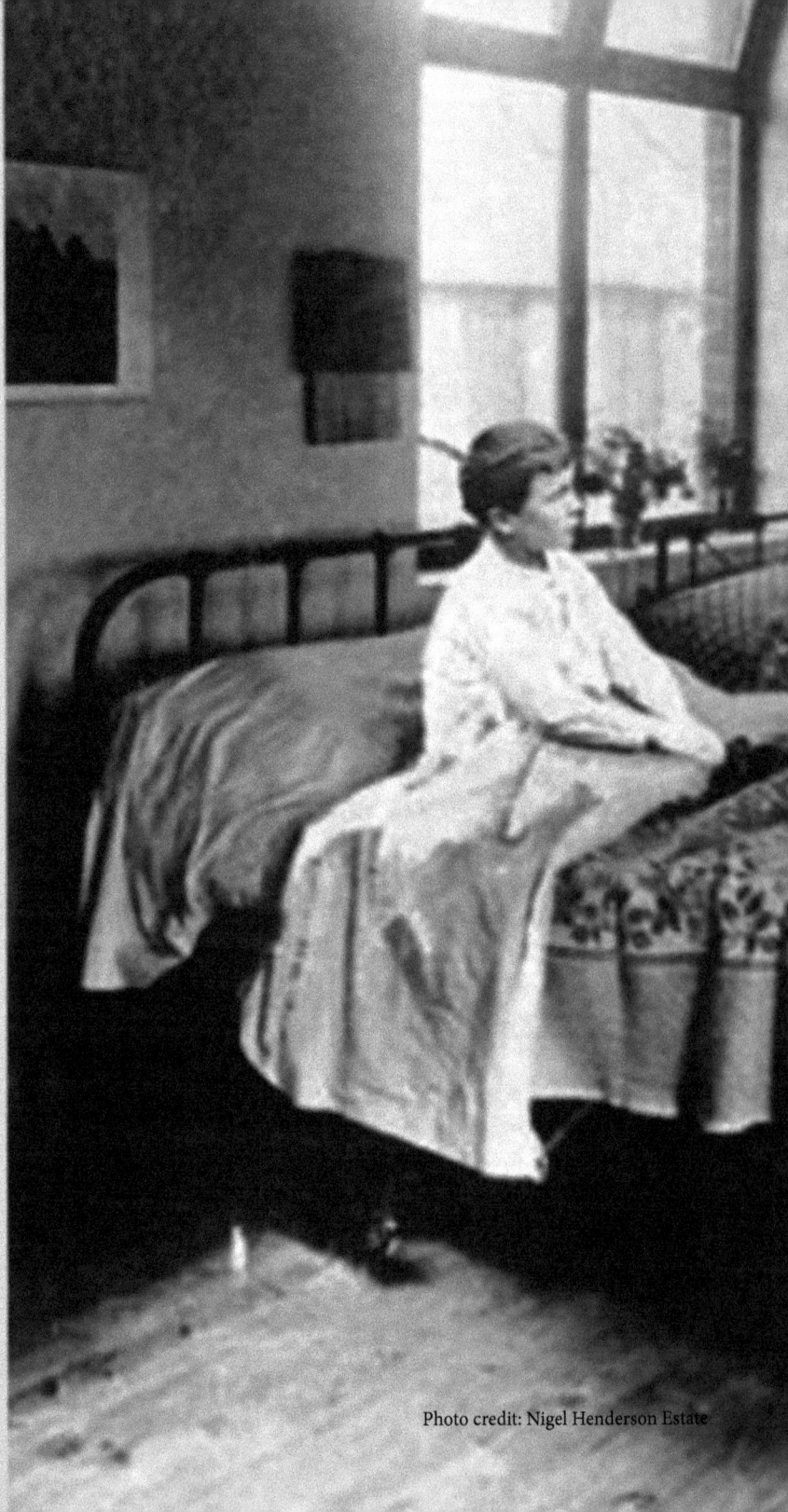

My parents were distraught. They had sold their business, our home—everything—to make the journey and, due to the outbreak of World War One, getting passage later would be very difficult. Even if I lived, a typhoid diagnosis would prevent me from being permitted aboard any ship for many weeks.

Tearfully, my parents prayed asking Heavenly Father to help them know what to do. The answer was not an easy one. They felt they should take the other family members and go to America without me. This broke my parents' hearts—they didn't want to go if it meant leaving me behind. Worse, the thought of telling me their plan was almost unbearable to them.

Photo credit: Nigel Henderson Estate

When my parents suggested that the family might have to travel immediately, I was not afraid. "It's all right," I said. "You go now; I'll come later with the Elders" (American missionaries who would soon finish their South African missions).

With a promise from the missionaries that they would watch over me and bring me as soon as I was well, my parents and the rest of the family boarded a lumber ship and sailed for America.

No. 3366

PASSPORT.

We, Viscount Buxton, A Member of His Majesty's Most Honourable Privy Council, Knight Grand Cross of the Most Distinguished Order of St. Michael and St. George, High Commissioner for South Africa, Governor-General and Commander-in-Chief in and over the Union of South Africa.

Request and require in the Name of His [Majesty] whom it may concern to allow [Mr.] Martin, Wife & Seven Children [with]out let or hindrance, and to [afford] assistance and protection of [which he may] stand in need.

Pretoria,
January, 1916.

Buxton
Governor-General
Union of South Africa.

[By] His Excellency
[the Governor-]General.

[Signature]

[A]cting Secretary for the Interior.
for Minister of the Interior.

[This] is valid for two years only [from] issue. It may be renewed for [periods] of two years each, after which [a new passport will] be required.

ENDORSEMENTS.

DESCRIPTION OF BEARER.

Age 41. Profession Merchant

Place and date of birth England. 25/1/1875

Maiden name if widow, or married woman travelling singly.

Height 5 feet 9 inches.

Forehead Medium   Eyes (colour) Blue

Nose Small   Mouth Small

Chin Round   Colour of Hair Gray

Complexion Fresh   Face Round

Any special peculiarities —

National status a British Subject

PHOTOGRAPH OF BEARER.

Weeks later I was well enough to leave the hospital, but I wasn't very strong. The Elders had to prop me up between them so I looked healthy enough to board the ship.

We had fire drills often on the ship; there was concern that German military ships might hinder our voyage, but we saw no enemy vessels.

I got much stronger on the trip. Soon I was running around the deck. We sailed first to England to see my grandmother and cousins and then on to New York where we stopped for some amusement at Coney Island.

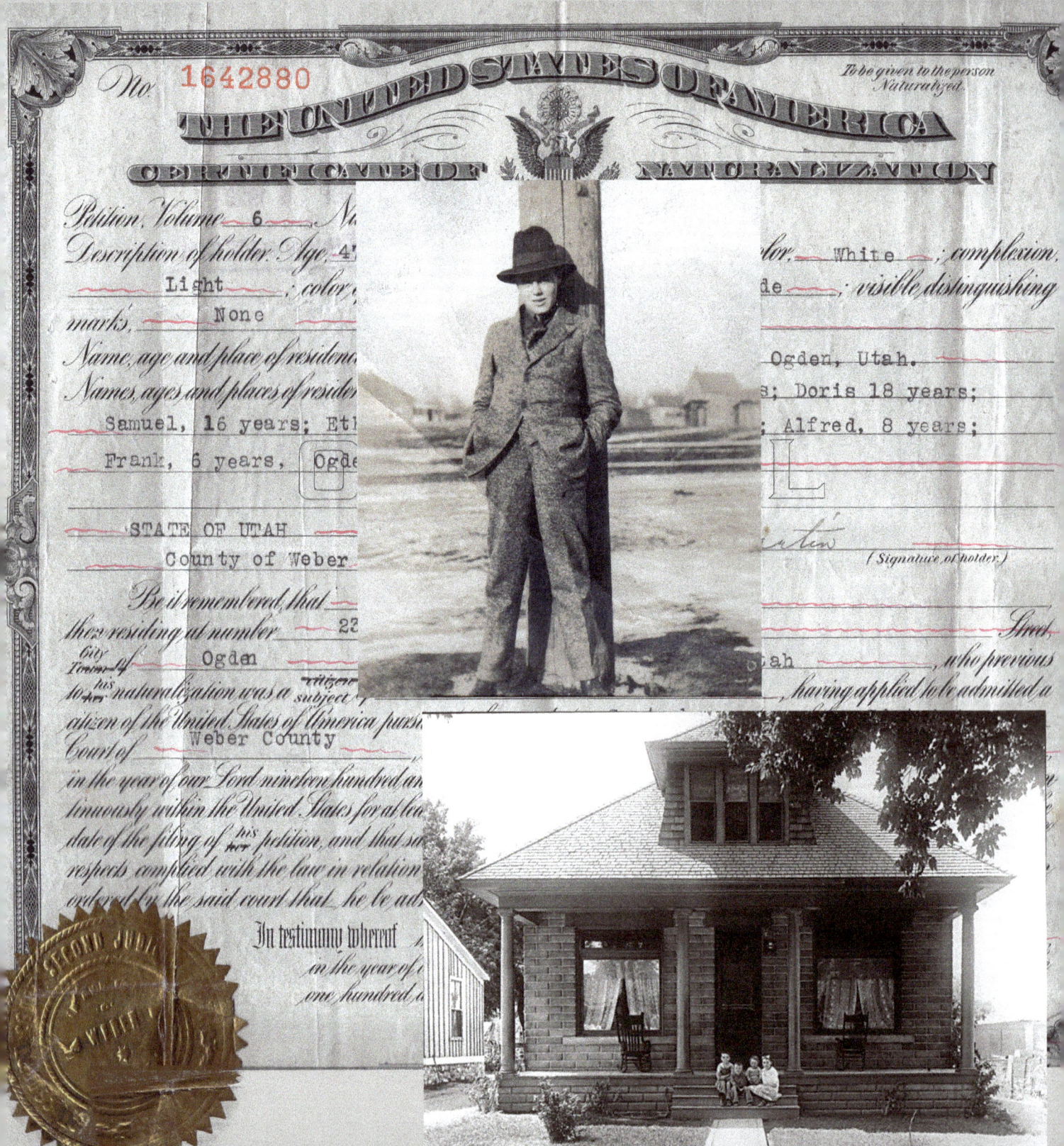

After a long train ride I was reunited with my family in Ogden Utah. My parents were overjoyed that I had recovered and made the journey without mishap.

Snow was a novelty to me—but I was soon sledding and skiing with the other kids in Utah.

Before my last year of high school, a friend of mine and I hopped onto a freight car of the Southern Pacific Railroad bound for San Francisco, California. We got jobs in a gold and silver smelter. Later we went to Washington State to work in a box factory. Then we took migrant jobs harvesting produce across the states to Wisconsin and then down to Iowa and Nebraska before returning to Utah for school. That was the hardest work I'd ever done!

After high school I sailed again on a boat to England to serve a two-year mission for the Lord. Then I sailed in a small fishing boat to Holland/The Netherlands and toured there—and a bit in Belgium and France.

Not long after returning to the United States, I got a job as a clerk for a small air transport company. I married my sweetheart and had two children. I had my first airplane ride in a small single engine airplane (that's me, playing pilot in the cockpit).

For many years afterward I worked for airlines—and got to sail through the air to Europe, Asia, and back to South Africa. What a life!

HOW MANY modes of transportation are shown/mentioned in the story? WHICH four continents are named? NAME six countries Samuel went to. WHAT seven U.S. states are mentioned? WHICH six cities are named? HOW MANY brothers and sisters did Sam have (see one below!)? WHAT are their names? WHERE are your ancestors from? (See FamilySearch.org.) Answers, online secrets, free multicultural ebooks, and lesson plans here: KidsWorldBooks.com/online-story-secrets

EPILOGUE

Sam loved golf and gin rummy. He learned to play the piano and played for services on his mission. Samuel's first wife, Ruth Wright, died of cancer in 1945. They had two children, Dean (who served a mission in South Africa) and Marilyn (Woodruff). Sam married Jean Homolka in Chicago in 1947. Sam worked for United Airlines for 42 years. By the time he retired in 1969, he was the assistant to the president of the company. Sam served as a special field representative of the Genealogical Society of Utah, helping to collect family records for people in many places. He died in 1983.

Sources: Samuel P. Martin's autobiography, Samuel Martin & Clara Ashford Martin (autobiography and biography), Ethel M. Beckstrand personal history. (The image on the cover is actually of Sam's youngest brother, Frank [with Samuel's face added]! See the back to see Frank's face. Get all four Young American Immigrants books: KidsWorldBooks.com)

www.ingramcontent.com/pod-product-compliance
Lightning Source LLC
Chambersburg PA
CBHW041216240426
43661CB00012B/1061